WICCA

FINDING

YOUR PATH

*A Beginner's Guide to Wiccan
Traditions, Solitary Practitioners, Eclectic
Witches, Covens, and Circles*

BY LISA CHAMBERLAIN

Published by **Wicca Shorts**

ISBN: 1522990593

ISBN-13: 978-1522990598

Disclaimer

No part of this publication may be reproduced or transmitted in any form or by any means, mechanical or electronic, including photocopying or recording, or by any information storage and retrieval system, or transmitted by email without permission in writing from the publisher.

While all attempts have been made to verify the information provided in this publication, neither the author nor the publisher assumes any responsibility for errors, omissions, or contrary interpretations of the subject matter herein.

This book is for entertainment purposes only. The views expressed are those of the author alone, and should not be taken as expert instruction or commands. The reader is responsible for his or her own actions.

Adherence to all applicable laws and regulations, including international, federal, state, and local governing professional licensing, business practices, advertising, and all other aspects of doing business in the US, Canada, or any other jurisdiction is the sole responsibility of the purchaser or reader.

Neither the author nor the publisher assumes any responsibility or liability whatsoever on the behalf of the purchaser or reader of these materials.

Any perceived slight of any individual or organization is purely unintentional.

YOUR FREE GIFT

As a way of showing my appreciation for purchasing my book, I'm giving away an exclusive, free eBook to my readers—*Wicca: Little Book of Wiccan Spells*.

The book is ideal for any Wiccans who want to start practicing magic. It contains a collection of ten spells that I have deemed suitable for beginners.

You can download it by visiting:

www.wiccaliving.com/bonus

I hope you enjoy it.

CONTENTS

INTRODUCTION

Despite the many social inroads made by Wiccans and other witches over the last few decades, confusion and stereotypes about this rich and unique religious belief system still persist in our mainstream culture.

Those who are brave enough to declare themselves witches are often still met with stares of disbelief, outright laughter, or concerned questioning about their mental state, even from well-meaning friends.

Yes, there are still plenty among us who think that witches are only fictional characters from fairy tales, movies, and books. And despite the better reputation that our more contemporary fictional witches (and "wizards") have been getting, many people still associate the "w" word with wicked intentions and evil deeds.

But those who take the time to explore Wicca with an open mind will always discover that Wiccan witches follow an ethical moral code, which can be summed up simply as "harm none."

And this is only one way in which actual witches—Wiccan or non-Wiccan—defy the old stereotypes. Wiccans are not malicious supernatural beings flying around on broomsticks and boiling reptiles in cauldrons. Wiccans are healers, soothsayers, wise-women and wise-men, spiritual counselors, herbalists, gardeners, astrologers, animal-lovers, and, just like every single being on Earth, inherently part of the divine.

Welcome to this introductory guide to the practice of Wicca, an earth-based religion of polytheistic pagan worship, reverence for nature, and magical witchcraft.

While Wicca is a modern religion, it is based on and inspired by pre-Christian pagan practices, often referred to by participants as "the Old Religion." It has many forms and traditions, most of which are also influenced by esoteric elements of the Western Mystery Tradition as it was developed in the Middle Ages, including the mystical philosophy of the Kabbalah, alchemy, the role of the Elements, and more.

Some forms of Wicca also make use of older systems of astrology, and even divination practices like Tarot cards and runes.

Then, of course, there's magic (or "magick" as many prefer to spell it), which, for those who practice it, goes hand-in-hand with the concepts and tenets held within the Wiccan belief system.

Now would be a good time to point out that not all Wiccans practice magic, and not all consider themselves to be "witches."

However, since the original practitioners of what we now call Wicca did both, this guide considers Wiccans in general to be witches who practice magic, with all due respect to those who differ in these regards, and who are still considered to be included in this guide, which focuses on the wide variety of ways in which contemporary Wicca is practiced today.

Wicca began as a group-centered practice taking place within covens—a coven being, of course, a group or gathering of witches for the purpose of conducting ritual or magic.

These covens originally operated in secrecy—and many still do—in keeping with the idea that witches had been meeting in such a way, secretly, throughout the Christianization of Europe and the persecution of pagans that followed.

While it later turned out that this wasn't exactly the case, the new-found "tradition" of covens proved very beneficial to the growth of witchcraft in its revived form. Witches coming together in covens to study their Craft, create and adapt new practices, and spread their knowledge to others was indeed the vehicle for the rise of Wicca, first in Europe and then in the United States and beyond.

This guide will, of course, cover the basic institution of the coven, but will also introduce you to the wider spectrum of contemporary Wiccan practice, moving from the traditional, "orthodox" covens to looser, more "eclectic" covens and circles, and then on to the more recent phenomenon of solitary practice, which has appealed to both traditional and eclectic Wiccans alike.

You will also be introduced to a handful of the main Wiccan traditions practiced today, as well as the concept of eclectic Wicca, which has been the fastest growing form over the past few decades. If you don't already have a sense of the amazing diversity of this innovative religion, you certainly will by the end of this book!

Whether you're considering pursuing Wicca as a spiritual path, or would simply like to know more about it, this guide is a great place to start.

As a matter of fact, Wicca is one of the world's few religions that is as likely to be studied entirely on one's own through reading as through in-person guidance from other practitioners. Unlike a sect of Christianity or Judaism, for example, there aren't a lot of opportunities to sit in on a religious service to see what it's like.

Depending on where you live, you might be able to find a Wiccan circle or even an "open" coven where you can witness a sabbat celebration or other ritual, but if not, you're pretty much on your own.

Of course, the Internet provides plenty of resources and opportunities to discuss the Craft with others, and this has proved immensely valuable to new and experienced Wiccans alike. But do be aware that the open, "democratic" nature of the Internet has its drawbacks—chiefly that anyone can present any information they like, whether it's accurate or not.

The best way to make sure you're getting a solid education in Wicca is to read widely and voraciously, but it's equally important to pay attention to what your intuition is telling you as you absorb the information. The reason there are so many forms of Wicca is that there are countless ways to understand and experience its core essence, and it will likely take a while for you to discover where your individual path begins.

As you grow in your knowledge and experience of the Craft, you just may find that it has become more than an interest in a religion, but a rewarding way of life. May everything that you read within be of service to you on your journey, and let love and light guide you toward the path that is best for you.

Blessed Be.

WITCHCRAFT: A BRIEF OVERVIEW OF HISTORY AND SECRECY

The use of witchcraft goes back as far as the outer edges of our human record, and probably farther. It is possibly as old as civilization itself.

In 3100 B.C., ancient Egyptians worshiped under a polytheistic belief system, and we have evidence that this included sorcery. In the pre-Christian worlds of the Norse, Celts, Greeks, Romans, and Indians, working with herbs, stones, and magic words was very commonplace, as was a visit to a seer to ask questions about how a battle, invasion, or life in general was going to turn out.

Flashing forward to the era when Jesus was alive, we can see that the magical arts were still widely practiced, as there are several references to them in the Bible.

And the witch trials in both Europe and the New World of the 16th and 17th centuries show the belief in witchcraft still going strong in the late Middle Ages—though by this time, of course, the way in which those who practiced the craft were viewed was distorted by religious propaganda and paranoia.

Indeed, the misrepresentation of witchcraft seems to be its own "tradition," going back, in some places, nearly two thousand years.

The leaders of the Roman Catholic Church needed to eradicate all forms of paganism in order for their own religion to truly take hold, and so gradually witchcraft became associated with the Christian ideas of "evil" and "Satan."

Thus, people who saw fit to continue practicing were forced to retreat under the hood of night for fear of being punished, excommunicated, or even worse, executed. It was an ugly time that all but eradicated the old ways, and secrecy is the only thing that kept its remnants alive.

Many modern covens and solitary witches have preserved this tradition of secrecy, believing that quiet and privacy for practitioners is still of utmost importance, and with good reason. Magic and rituals aren't a novelty, and their impact is far-reaching.

Besides, there is also a lingering fear of persecution in the community, which is surprising yet still common for Wiccans to endure. Indeed, mainstream views of witchcraft in modern times are also, unfortunately, still a bit muddled due to the false images of witches we see in movies, books, and other forms of media.

Even in a world where you can summon a Wiccan Priestess for your last rites in hospital, there are sneers and jeers. Many practitioners feel it is simply better just to keep quiet and do as one will.

Unfortunately, the secrecy of centuries past, plus the near-eradication of the old religion, means that we don't have a lot of concrete information about how our ancestors practiced what we now call witchcraft. We don't even know for sure exactly when or how covens came into the picture. While the first historical references we find to covens in the Western world date back to the 16th century, we just don't know much beyond that.

Nonetheless, the coven today is a long-revered institution that guards the secrets of the craft while ensuring its survival, and this is thanks to the work of the spiritual pioneers of the late 19th and early 20th centuries.

THE BIRTH OF WICCA

The late 19th century saw the revival of a variety of occult arts in Britain, where many spiritual enthusiasts met, exchanged ideas, and formed groups and societies for the purpose of further pursuing their interests.

One such group was the Hermetic Order of The Golden Dawn, a kind of coven in its own right whose members studied and practiced magic as well as divination, contacting spirits, and all things esoteric.

The beginnings of modern Wicca really originated here, when the British occultist and author Aleister Crowley was taken under The Golden Dawn's wing in the early 1900s. Crowley's work and writings became highly influential for another occultist who came along a few decades later—Gerald Gardner.

Gerald Gardner is considered to be the "father of modern witchcraft." Others call him the "grandfather of Wicca." He was a British occult enthusiast and writer who trained under the Rosicrucian Order, where he met a few friends who ultimately introduced him to a group called the New Forest Coven, into which he was initiated.

From these coveners, whose identities remain mysterious today, Gardner learned rituals, magic, and other lore dating back to earlier times. He combined this with the inspiration he drew from the writings of Aleister Crowley to start his own coven, which he called Bricket Wood.

Over the next few years, he developed his framework for witchcraft which we now call Gardnerian Wicca. And although the full extent of the specific beliefs, rituals, and other practices involved in Traditional Gardnerian Wicca are known only to initiates of Gardnerian covens—in keeping with the tradition of secrecy—it is this framework that much of modern Wiccan practice is based on, whether it's coven-based, solitary, or even eclectic.

WICCA TRADITIONS

From Gardner's form of the craft (which he never called "Wicca," by the way—that came later), other traditions developed. Initiates in Gardner's lineage went on to form Alexandrian and Seax Wicca, just to name a couple.

The continuing development of this very diverse religion has gotten to the point where there are probably more Wiccan paths than can be described in one book—particularly if you include eclectic practitioners in the mix. However, those new to the Craft who are reading around on the Internet and in print are most likely to encounter one of three main "branches" on the tree of Wicca—Gardnerian, Alexandrian, or Dianic—either in their "pure form" or in forms loosely based on the original.

These three, along with a few other more commonly encountered traditions, will be discussed in further detail later in this guide.

What's the difference between one tradition and another?

Each Wiccan tradition has its own way of practicing the religion: the protocols for rituals, the deities to worship, the structure of worship, how a coven is organized, and any number of other details large and small may differ from one tradition to the next.

Two Wiccan traditions may have some of the same things in common, such as a similar way to begin a sabbat ritual, but differ widely in other ways, such as the pantheon their patron deities are selected from.

While there are set rules in each tradition, it's generally understood that covens and solitary practitioners alike may add to the tradition's teachings and adapt the rules as necessary, so long as the tradition's main teachings remain intact. This will depend on how "orthodox" the coven or solitary prefers to be.

Of course, once too many changes are made, the tradition is no longer being followed, which means it's likely that a new tradition is being formed.

Do I have to follow a specific tradition?

In essence, all Wiccans use the work and beliefs of one tradition or another, at least to some extent.

Unless you're literally making up every single aspect of your practice (in which case, you're not actually practicing Wicca), then you're following in the footsteps of those who came before you.

That being said, there's a lot of variety in terms of how strictly any given Wiccan adheres to the "way it's always been" along a particular path.

Covens typically follow specific Wiccan traditions that dictate their structure, rituals, and spell-work. While covens tend to adhere pretty strictly to their tradition, they may from time to time make exceptions, but this will depend on a unique set of circumstances that prevail in the group.

Solitary practitioners also follow traditions. Some follow a specific tradition as closely as they can, while other prefer to put their own twist on older versions of practice.

Some people follow many different aspects of several traditions, preferring to mix and match. This is called Eclectic Wicca, something that we'll look deeper at a little later.

Finding and following a tradition in Wicca is a wonderful thing because it's a way to learn and grow into your shoes, so to speak. It can be a great feeling to know that you found the right religion for you, and this is what following a tradition can provide.

Sometimes there can be some trial and error involved, though. If you're checking out a coven in your area and find that the tradition the coven is following isn't exactly what you had envisioned for yourself, simply search for other options and learn as much as you can along the way until you find the perfect fit.

That is, of course, one of the most appealing parts of being Wiccan: the ability to adapt and grow into the right path. You may even find yours by starting with an established tradition, and then moving on to your own eclectic practice. This approach is great for the independently-minded newbie.

Just keep in mind that wherever your ultimate path leads you, knowledge is crucial, so you should always be willing to learn—whether it be from books like this one, or from a coven or circle in your area. We'll take a closer look at these "in-person" options in the next few sections of this guide.

COVENS, CIRCLES, AND SOLITARY PRACTITIONERS

AN INTRODUCTION TO COVENS

Because covens seem to be the most complex of the many ways that Wiccans practice, this is a good time to look deeper into these rather secretive groups.

Yes, covens are still usually secretive, both in the spirit of tradition and as a way to protect the energy and activity in their circles from interference from the outside world.

So what exactly is a coven? What do its members do? How do covens work, and why do so many people gravitate towards them? Is it wise to join a coven, and if you do, what are the benefits and potential pitfalls of doing so?

These are all good questions. In this section, we'll be trying to answer them.

SPIRITUAL COMMUNITY AND TREASURE TROVE OF KNOWLEDGE

While the solitary and/or eclectic path has plenty of appeal, many people who are new to Wicca do seem inexplicably called to join a coven. So what is the pull?

Many feel that because the practice of gathering together for magical purposes was exercised back as far as ancient times, that this is the right way to observe such traditions. Others feel that joining a coven is an important part of becoming Wiccan and that the only way to become a Wiccan is through the most traditional of means possible. Furthermore, there are those who feel that they could benefit greatly from the knowledge and spiritual teachings of others and wish to congregate for the purpose of learning.

Each of these is a very valid reason for wishing to join and regularly attend the proceedings of a coven.

You might say that traditionalism and the conservation of old ways is held near and dear in terms of practicing most, if not all, religions.

Even the Roman Catholic Church has a hierarchical structure and a priesthood with an air of exclusivity. Convents are also much like covens, and some may even find it interesting that the two words have somewhat related etymologies. Buddhist monks gather for spiritual reasons and, like nuns, live together and dedicate their entire existence to learning the spiritual teachings of their chosen path. Then there are gurus and swamis, the ancient Druids, and a litany of many more spiritual societies.

Those practicing modern Paganism might consider the Druids to be a great example of a type of "coven before its time," given how much work was put into developing magical abilities, healing, and studying the mysteries hidden from plain view. Druids were not alone, however.

Shamans, herbalists, Native Americans, Ancient Egyptians, Greeks, and many more had fraternal orders that allowed for the working of magic as well as healing and worship of the divine.

Because we all want to be as close to our roots as possible, it makes perfect sense for Wiccans to seek to join covens in order to preserve a tradition that could very well be dying out due to the influx of solitary practitioners, eclectic Wiccans, and generalized circles popping up all over the place.

Covens do at times feel threatened by the impending extinction of their lines. Fortunately, there are plenty of newcomers to Wicca who are inclined to be purists when it comes to their religion. It's completely natural to want to fully immerse yourself in a new spiritual leaning. It's the only way for some, and this means seeking out a coven that is accepting new members and possibly even going through the same initiation rituals Gerald Gardner first introduced all those decades ago.

Purists, as we all know, are going to be driven in their purpose, learning as many of the old ways as possible because their general attitude is that joining a coven is the only right way to become Wiccan and sustain a 'true' Wiccan path. We know that this isn't true anymore, but if seeking out and joining a coven is what makes you feel the most at home in the faith, by all means do so. After all, there is no right or wrong way to follow this deeply spiritual and earth-attuned path.

Finally, we know that covens are treasure troves of information on the craft and its tenets. Their members join together and exchange knowledge, putting it all into practice, learning exponentially as the group gets older and wiser as a whole. Those looking to be formally initiated into covens may be enticed by the prospect of benefiting from this knowledge in their own solo work, in addition to their participation in the group.

While some see this as a selfish desire for personal gain, this is actually one of the reasons that covens bring in new members: to pass on the information and teachings they possess.

If the Hermetic Order of The Golden Dawn had never adopted Aleister Crowley into their circle, Gerald Gardner wouldn't have had so much magical inspiration and information to work with himself. The need to learn is within all of us, and that is never a selfish pursuit, so if this is your aim, you have arrived at the right place by looking into covens and what they do.

All of these are very good reasons to research covens and become a member of one. Without these motives, we wouldn't have these special spiritual societies in this day and age, and thus, this unique aspect of the faith would wither away into the past.

THE COVEN LIFE

Because of the tradition of secrecy in most covens, and because each coven is unique, it's a bit difficult to get into specific detail about what it's like to belong to one.

But by now, you at least know that a coven isn't just a bunch of cackling hags around a bubbling cauldron. A coven is a community of Wiccans who are dedicated to the Craft and its teachings, as well as, usually, a specific tradition of it.

These special groups are sometimes quite old, with lineage dating back as far as the 1960s, but there are always new groups developing as well, who carry on the old traditions while perhaps adding some of their own.

Covens perform a lot of great rituals, sabbats, and healing circles. They also do handfastings, naming ceremonies, and much more. They can heal people, hold prayer circles, and use their knowledge to spread love and light in the world around them.

TRADITIONAL COVEN STRUCTURES

The coven is traditionally made up of anywhere from nine to thirteen members, but in modern times, some groups like to allow larger numbers in order to include family members. Others keep their group smaller—with as few as three members—for a more intimate circle.

There is usually a hierarchical structure to traditional covens. Generally, there are "degrees," or ranks, that initiates can make their way through by studying and learning from elders in the Craft.

There are typically three different degrees, with the First being the most basic requirement for initiation. The Second and Third Degrees permit more responsibility and activity within the coven leadership.

The coven leader, or leaders, will make larger decisions affecting the coven and will preside over important rituals.

Typically, a more traditional coven will have one or two leaders. If there is only one, it will be a female who is referred to as the High Priestess.

The High Priestess is considered to be the center of all rituals and magic. She makes the coven's bigger decisions and evaluates prospective members to ensure that they are ready to enter initiation. She also decides whether members who want to pursue initiation into a higher degree are ready to do so.

If there is a second leader, it will be a male who is referred to as the High Priest. Traditionally, the High Priest was subordinate to the High Priestess, and this is still true in some covens, but many, even those who descend from the original Gardnerian and Alexandrian traditions, have opted for a more equal sharing of power between their leaders.

The High Priest and Priestess are highly knowledgeable in the craft and may be elders in the group. They may have even have come up through the ranks of the coven themselves, if the coven has been around long enough, finally reaching the top level of leadership.

Just beneath the High Priest and Priestess are the members of the Inner Court.

The Inner Court is the group of witches who have completed at least the Second Degrees of initiation and have proven themselves wholly proficient in both their ritual and spell-work.

The Third Degree Practitioners are the ones who are most well-versed and are being positioned to start and manage a coven of their own, if they desire to do so. These witches are closest to the leaders and are often present in the sacred circle during specific rituals and magic undertakings. They also help to teach the people in the coven's Outer Circle who are seeking First Degree initiation.

Second Degree initiates are at a level where they are allowed to be a part of the circle and are deepening their knowledge of the coven's ritual work while helping with the non-initiates. They are taught by the Priestess and Third Degree members at an accelerated rate, illustrating the importance of their role in the coven. Some Second Degree witches will even have the ability to train First Degrees if they have proven themselves ready. This could also indicate a Second Degree witch who is ready for initiation into the Third Degree.

Speaking of this type of advancement, it's useful to note that one of the big taboos in many covens with hierarchies is when a Second Degree initiate asks to be moved up to the final level, rather than being invited.

This major faux pas may even see you removed from the coven if the Priestess is upset enough (although it would be hard to imagine, it does happen. Hierarchy can have interesting effects on the human ego).

The First Degree witches are those who have just been initiated into the craft. They are in a rank of their own, separate from both the Outer and Inner Circles.

First Degree practitioners have shown that they are pure in intention, that they have the desire and passion to learn, and have a basic understanding of magic and rituals. This level of initiation allows members to learn how to cast a circle in their particular coven, undergoing training from those in the higher ranks. Once they have proven themselves proficient and dedicated, they may be initiated into the Second Degree, but as with all levels, only with the Priestess's blessing.

The Outer Circle is occupied by those who would like to be initiated into the coven. They are not present for everything that the coven does, often being closed out of more important or sacred rituals and esbats. This is to protect the coven from those with ill intentions or those who are simply not ready to begin progressing on their path.

In the Outer Circle, one is still in the process of becoming educated and proving of one's self to the coven and its leader(s). They are not always even considered to be "members" until they are initiated into the First Degree, and they cannot enter the First Degree unless the higher ranks approve.

Looking at this rigid structure, one can see how serious and devout coven members must be to become a part of the main circle. It may seem rather elaborate, but this is the traditional structure that covens followed back in the early days of Wicca.

There are many groups that still observe this hierarchy today, although others have simplified things a bit. It all depends on the coven's tradition and the preferences of the coveners.

NEWER ADAPTATIONS

In terms of equality and views of power structures, the world has come a long way since the mid-1950s when the traditional coven structure was ingrained into modern witchcraft.

In the decades since, and particularly in the 21st century, many Wiccans have adapted the old rules to make them more practical and appropriate to their own experience of society.

For example, the traditional supremacy of the High Priestess was meant, in part, to balance out the gender inequalities of British society in the middle of the last century. While it can be argued that the world still has a long way to go toward achieving total equality, many contemporary Wiccans have come to see this aspect of the traditional coven structure as unnecessary and even cumbersome. Therefore, the High Priestess and High Priest may share power equally in many modern-day covens.

Another variation is the complete and total abolishing of degrees. This makes for fewer issues among the ranks because, well, there are none. It also prevents dissent that can arise from feeling pinned under such a limiting authority figure of sorts. Without degrees, people feel more at ease to practice and learn at their own pace instead of trying to cram three centuries' worth of information into their brains in order to make the next rank.

Moreover, some covens do not allow for an Outer Circle. The High Priestess may interview perspective members or the coven may advertise when it is open to new initiates, closing itself off from new memberships for a large majority of the time. This keeps all of the coven's proceedings from being seen by people who might decide not to join, but will still know about—and might even go around speaking of—details relating to of the coven's work.

Another system that people find preferable over the traditional coven structure is an electoral system, whereby the High Priest and Priestess are voted on by the members of the coven.

This can be tricky, depending on the maturity level of all the egos involved, because influence may have nothing to do with who is most deserving or learned. However, when members are being responsible and letting divine forces inform their decisions, the results can be very satisfying.

As you can see, there are several different possibilities for how a given coven is structured and operated.

The extent to which hierarchy is observed is one of the things you'll want to inquire about when looking into joining a coven. You'll also want to know about the general rules and requirements.

It tends to go without saying that coven members are expected to attend every meeting and every ritual (at least, those which they are permitted to attend, depending on their rank). They may also be restricted to practicing magic within the coven's circle alone, prohibited from doing their own solo work until initiated into a higher level (or, in some covens, not at all). Each group will conduct all of its rituals in a specific way that is traditional to their circle, and some will only allow one copy of the coven's Book of Shadows to exist.

Of course some covens are much more rule-oriented than others, but because all are closed to the public, there is no way of knowing just how strict a given coven may be until you approach them with your interest in joining. Before you start knocking on doors, however, it's useful to take a closer look at the benefits and potential drawbacks of choosing this path of Wiccan practice.

THE PROS AND CONS OF COVENS

As with any decision involving spirituality, the choice of whether or not to join a coven should not be taken lightly.

Coven membership is a serious commitment, and it requires careful consideration. You will have to be honest with yourself about whether you are willing to go the distance.

Even if it sounds like a very exciting idea at first, it is important to evaluate each potential advantage and each possible drawback before you can be certain whether coven life is for you.

THE BENEFITS OF JOINING A COVEN

Becoming a member of a coven can bring many blessings that may end up being very important to your spiritual path.

Perhaps the main benefit of joining a coven is the obvious acceleration in learning. You will be training yourself in Wicca actively, learning each and every skill the coven views as essential.

In addition, a number of knowledgeable members with unique perspectives on the Craft will be taking you under their wing, which means you have the potential to learn a very diverse skill set.

Many coven members like the sense of community that a coven can provide. It gives them a feeling of belonging in a world that isn't entirely open to the tenets of Wicca. As just about anyone in the faith can tell you, it can feel a tad lonely to be the only Wiccan in a room of Christians and Atheists.

Being a part of a coven gives Wiccan practitioners something to belong to and somewhere to practice their religion with others who share a common spiritual orientation. This sense of community is really no different from what Christians, Muslims, and Jews enjoy in their own congregations.

Some hold the view that the magic worked as part of a coven is much more powerful than that of a solitary practitioner. This is why people so often form circles (groups that are their own entity separate from covens) for doing rituals and spell-work.

This may or may not be true, depending on how intent and focused the group is and whether the work is really done correctly. If you consider the potential power of the raising of energy in covens, it could be really quite spectacular, but that doesn't necessarily mean that the energy raised by a solitary witch is any less authentic.

Others like to be led by someone with a vast amount of wisdom, and find that being a part of a coven allows them to do so freely without having to do the heavy thinking for the group. There is also a lesson in commitment here that people enjoy learning. This is something that covens teach through mandatory attendance, a vow of secrecy, and a hierarchical structure to make one's way up through.

THE DRAWBACKS OF WORKING IN A COVEN

Those who have tried covens and found it not to be their best option have tended to feel a lack of spiritual freedom. Some would even go far enough to call it dogma.

Being a part of a coven can mean following a very rigid system where everything must be done a certain way. Its members can also be less than forgiving of those who break any of the rules, as they are seen to be going against the coven and betraying trust.

So you may have to weigh "the good of the group" against your own personal preferences at times, and not all aspiring Wiccans are quite cut out for this way of being.

Some covens don't actually allow many, or any, of their members to progress beyond a specific degree, preventing them from being able to leave the group and start their own coven or even having an intimate part in rituals and spell-work. In fact, certain covens don't allow for spell-casting outside of their circle, figuratively and spiritually cutting members off at the knees and keeping them at arm's length from the Goddess and God.

This is much like what cults and even some churches do to their followers and should be a red flag for anyone wishing to truly progress along their spiritual path.

Because attendance is generally mandatory for anyone who is initiated into a coven, it can be difficult to wedge coven participation into one's lifestyle. Not everyone can commit to something that requires them to come out for every esbat, sabbat, and spell-casting there is in a year, so it is best to consider this in terms of practicality.

Can you attend every meeting a coven holds in addition to taking care of all of your other commitments?

If not, you may need to reduce your other activities to create a less hectic life—which isn't a bad idea for anyone, really—or else stick to the solitary path. (Another option is to join a circle, rather than a coven, as circles usually have less demanding requirements. Circles will be discussed in the next section, below.)

Finally, some find it difficult to feel an intimate level of connection with their spell and ritual work if they are a part of a group, as they don't feel to be "in the driver's seat" of their own spiritual path.

This is another potential reason to try a circle first, to see if you can work with others and still feel as connected and focused on the earth and your task.

SOME GENTLE WORDS OF CAUTION

Even though we live in a world where religion should be a safe thing to come together for, there are some unscrupulous people out there who will engage in unethical and even dangerous activities in the name of Wicca.

Unfortunately, you do have to take some important precautions when it comes to looking into covens. If you are becoming a part of one and notice any of the following behaviors on the part of your would-be fellow coveners, you are strongly advised to leave the group immediately. Depending on the circumstances, you may even want to report certain activities to the police.

Cult-like Atmosphere or Proceedings

If you find that the coven you have joined seems more interested in worshiping its leaders rather than the God and Goddess, it might be time to go before you're trapped in something you cannot get out of.

Cult leaders always start out appearing to be about a religion or spiritual path, but end up being about absolute control over their followers. Cults can be dangerous when people are brainwashed into doing risky and/or illegal things or giving up everything they have to a leader.

Satanic and Malevolent Work

Wicca is a religion of Threefold Law, and there should never be a situation where a coven is doing a spell that will harm anyone or anything.

The same goes for anything resembling "devil-worship" (Wiccans do not classically believe in "Satan") and/or making "sacrifices."

If you witness anything like this, turn around and walk in the other direction.

Covens that participate in these kinds of works are not Wiccan and can really destroy your life with their dark magic and poor reputations.

While there are NeoPagan groups who worship a deity named Satan in a pre-Biblical sense, Satanism is not Wicca and should not be confused with the Goddess-and-God-worshipping path.

Illegal Activities and Drug-Taking

If you find yourself in the middle of a "coven" gathering where there is illegal activity happening, this is a good time to remove yourself from their company.

Theft and vandalism are not a part of Wicca and go against its tenets, but unfortunately there are occasional miscreants who try to use the secrecy of coven work as a smokescreen to hide their juvenile antics.

As for drug use, it isn't ever a good idea to take something that someone gives to you unless you know exactly what's in it and what it's for.

Although some Pagan and NeoPagan groups use entheogenic drugs to attain heightened states of consciousness, taking drugs is dangerous, not to mention illegal, and you never know what you could be in for once they kick in.

Sexual Assault

Although many covens no longer operate in the nude or re-enact the union of the God and Goddess physically, some do, and so they often attract people with the wrong motives.

It's also possible that the use of ritual nudity and/or ritual sex is kept secret from new members, who will find the coven very appealing until it starts to get weird. Never become or remain a part of a coven where this kind of stuff is taking place (unless you're entirely comfortable with it), and if you witness anything physical happening against anyone's will, report it to the police.

Note: *These warnings may seem stern, but unfortunately they've been proven necessary through experience. They are not intended to scare you out of looking into initiation through a coven, however. Certainly, not every coven out there is a cult or a dangerous place to lure women and minors to—the incidents described above represent a very small minority. Nonetheless, it's always better to be safe than sorry, so keep your sixth sense primed for anything that seems off about a group you come into contact with.*

THE WICCAN CIRCLE: AN ALTERNATIVE TO THE COVEN

You may or may not have heard of "circles" before in your explorations of Wicca.

A circle is much like a coven in that it is a group of people coming together for the purpose of ritual worship and spellwork. It is also a big place of learning, both for newcomers to the Craft and for solitaries who are looking to find a sense of community in their practice.

This relatively new form of spiritual community has evolved out of a desire for less structure and less hierarchy than what is typically experienced in a traditional coven.

While you may see both circles and covens advertised in the same sections of online forums and directories, there are significant differences between these two types of Wiccan groups.

For starters, covens are generally exclusive, and often are not open to new members. You typically can't just arrange to come in and be a part of a coven. A circle is much more open, with fluctuating membership, usually allowing new people to come and go in order to see if it is something they enjoy. In addition, circles tend not to follow a specific tradition. Some do, and they may ask that only those who practice under their tradition, or else are willing to learn, join them, but usually they're fairly eclectic groups that come together from many different traditions and backgrounds.

As indicated above, circles are much more informal than traditional covens. Circles come together to practice the Craft, but without developing any hierarchy among members. No initiation is required, and there are no degrees to move through. There are no High Priestesses or High Priests. Attendance at meetings and rituals is not mandatory. A circle is more like a club, which makes many people feel more at ease and in control of their own spiritual paths.

Of course, for some Wiccans, a "club" is a little *too* loose in terms of the bonds that can be formed through the long-term commitment involved in a coven. Having consistent membership creates a more solid group dynamic than might be possible in a circle. Nonetheless, circles can be an ideal way for solitary and eclectic witches to come together and discuss their religion with like-minded others, to have access to community for ritual and spellwork, and to keep learning as they pursue their path.

SOLITARY PRACTICE

As the name would imply, solitary practitioners are Wiccans who choose to practice the Craft on their own—in their homes, backyards, or out in nature.

While some coven members may do spellwork on their own, if their coven permits it, this is not the same thing as solitary practice. Though they may occasionally join a circle for a particular sabbat celebration or other special occasion, the vast majority of a solitary Wiccan's spiritual work is done alone, and there are plenty who never commune with others at all.

It's estimated that more than half of all Wiccans are solitary practitioners.

This trend came about toward the end of the 20th century, when interest in Wicca had become widespread thanks to many published books on the Craft. For many would-be practitioners, there wasn't a coven within 500 miles, or if there was, it either wasn't open to new membership, or just wasn't a good fit in terms of personalities.

So people began practicing on their own, leaving behind the notion that one could only become a Wiccan through initiation by another Wiccan. Instead, they began to self-initiate, and adapt other coven practices for solitary use.

REASONS FOR CHOOSING A SOLITARY PATH

With the explosion of interest in Wicca in the age of the Internet, there are now many, many more covens out there in the world than there were just a few decades ago.

Nonetheless, there still isn't one in every single community, and again, even if there is one in your area, it may not be open to new members. Even if it is open, it may not be in the tradition you follow, or it may just not be a group you feel right about joining.

But lack of access to the coven of one's choice aside, there are several reasons why so many Wiccans choose a solitary path over a group pursuit.

For some, it really comes down to practicality. Frankly, it's much easier and more convenient to practice at home.

Gardnerian followers appreciate the freedom and comfort of working sky-clad for rituals, by themselves in their circle, with no prying eyes or inhibitions clouding their work. This also goes for witches who might be self-conscious in their ritual robes if others were to see them. In fact, for many solitaries, there's a lot to be said for the privacy of practicing behind closed doors.

It also works for those who have tight schedules and can't commit to the mandatory attendance expected of coven members—especially those with children.

You may remember that covens gather for spellwork, sabbats, and full moons, and sometimes new moons and special ceremonies. Not everyone can accommodate all of those occasions in addition to attending to the mundane events of life. Solitary practice allows for a 'when time allows' approach, and in this fast-paced world, this is a strong selling point for Wiccans who are up to their ears in life.

There's also the fact that solitaries can keep their faith entirely secret from the rest of the world, if they wish. Some Wiccans still have a lot of trepidation about identifying publicly with their religion, for fear of embarrassment, stigma, or other kinds of repercussions. While covens do practice secrecy, there's still no absolute guarantee that one would never be "outed" as a witch.

For other solitaries, the main attraction is freedom—to explore different traditions, to identify their own beliefs, to practice the kind of magic they want, and to basically just do their own thing.

In covens, rituals are usually set in stone, performed exactly according to the tradition's ways (with perhaps a few minor tweaks). In the solitary experience, rituals and spell-work can be much more fluid, with individual changes that would not be permitted in the more orthodox Wiccan traditions. On your own, you can decide for yourself how and where you cast a circle and the tools you use within it, and no one is there to tell you you're doing it incorrectly.

This also goes for pantheons and deities. There are a great many practitioners out there who crave the freedom to work the pantheon and/or deities they find to be most inspiring and evocative. When work within a coven, you are generally expected to follow their set of deities and their concept of the divine.

If you're fortunate enough to belong to a coven or circle that does share the same beliefs and ideas, that's wonderful, but this isn't always the case, and you can't force yourself to believe in something that doesn't feel right. Sometimes breaking away from the group is the only way to achieve your personal spiritual goals.

Finally, some believe that their energy is much more focused in their work when they do it alone.

It might be simply too distracting for practitioners to work with a group—there's a lot of activity going on when a coven performs a ritual or ceremonial magic. Others feel that their personal interests are not addressed by the group, or that the spellwork isn't personal because it is a collective effort towards one goal that they don't feel has anything to do with their lives. Service to others and to the greater world is good, but doing magic to effect change in one's own life is important too. Some solitary witches would simply prefer to work alone and focus their energy with laser-like precision on more personal pursuits or causes dear to their own hearts.

Solitary practice doesn't have to be a life-long commitment, though. You can always progress from working alone to joining your energies with like-minded others.

However, it can be a great place to start. If you are just beginning, you may find yourself unsure about which (if any) specific tradition you'd like to follow. The solitary approach means that you have the teachings and philosophies of several traditions at your fingertips. In fact, many coven members recommend spending time researching and studying on your own before deciding to join with others in your practice, so you start off with a clearer sense of what's right for you.

All in all, solitary practice has fewer rules in general. You can make and keep your own Book of Shadows, practice where and when you please, perform rituals to your liking, cast spells in the manner you feel most powerful, and worship the deities that you feel most at home with. You may not have the fellowship of others, but you are the leader of your own path.

Indeed, without the constraints of following a coven's rules and practices, the journey becomes a tailor-made experience.

SOME CONSIDERATIONS FOR THE SOLITARY PRACTITIONER

As you've no doubt concluded by now, solitary practice really is a completely different life from that of coven membership.

Being on one's own means grappling with and addressing certain aspects of the path in a different way. Here are some of the main elements of solitary practice that can present a challenge, at least at the beginning of the path.

Ethical Clarity

Although there's much more flexibility involved in practicing as a solitary versus as a coven member, this doesn't mean that it's a big free-for-all in terms of how one goes about the business of working magic.

Solitary practitioners are just as subject to the main Laws of Wicca as any member of a coven—namely, the Threefold Law and that very important line from the Wiccan Rede, "an it harm none."

"An it harm none, do what ye will" is generally considered to be the first rule of Wicca, and has often been presented as the only true rule. It means that as long as your actions do no harm to anyone—whether we're talking about spellwork or just how you go about your everyday life—then you should do what you want to do.

It's against Wiccan principles to work negative magic, of course, but it's also no good to work any kind of manipulative magic—in other words, anything that would interfere with another person's free will. If you think about it, you wouldn't want someone else doing anything to control your life or your actions, so it only makes sense that you shouldn't, either.

And for Wiccans who may be tempted to break, or even bend, this rule, the Threefold Law is there to make them think twice.

The Threefold Law, simply put, states that anything that you think, say, and do is sent out into the universe and then comes back at you three times as positively or negatively as the original thought, word, or action.

It can be likened to a ripple effect on a pond when a drop of rain hits it. At first, the circular ripples are very small, but they grow and spread out to become hundreds of times bigger than the very first ring. And when they reach the shore, they "bounce" off it and make their return journey back toward the center.

The same is true of how magical intentions operate on the spiritual plane. Understanding the Threefold Law is crucial to working successful magic without bringing negative consequences into your life.

Keeping this ripple metaphor in mind, there's also the need to remember that spellwork affects the entire Universe—not just the spellcaster or its intended recipient (if there is one).

It may not seem like the spellwork of one person could affect people down the street, in the next community, or across the world, but in actuality, one small incantation or knot tied at your altar could potentially have effects on those around you. This is why so many Wiccans use the phrase "harm to none" when sealing their magical work.

One potential challenge then, for solitary practitioners, is the ability to think through their spellwork through before setting anything in motion that they cannot take back.

It's important to be very clear about one's motives and expectations in magical work. This can be difficult when you're wrapped up in emotions, or stressed out by a situation, and can't discern whether or how to try to solve a problem through magic.

Having no one to talk to about it can make the issue all that more challenging.

This doesn't mean that coven work is automatically fail-safe in the ethics department—Wiccans can go awry in groups just as easily as on their own—but that the perspectives and experiences of others can help refine one's magical choices.

Following Tradition

While many Wiccans choose the solitary path in order to create their own entirely unique practice, there are plenty others who still wish to follow a specific tradition, whether it be Gardnerian, Alexandrian, or even an offshoot of one of these.

Although most existing traditions were by and large built around covens—particularly Gardnerian and Alexandrian Wicca—they can, and have been, adapted for solitary practice. The challenges in doing so are that it can be harder to learn on one's own, even with the best of books, and there are aspects of ritual that don't translate from a group setting to a circle of one.

Furthermore, there's bound to be aspects of the practice that just can't be known about unless you're a coven initiate. So solitaries may find themselves having to adapt their individual practice in order to find what works best for them.

Adaptation should not be confused with "cheating" or doing something incorrectly, however.

First, it's important to remember that even Gardner adapted his coven's ritual liturgy over time, and Alex Sanders actually made adaptability part of his tradition's philosophy.

In many ways, it could be argued that adaptation is part of the tradition of Wicca as a whole. As long as you're following your chosen tradition as faithfully as you can, there's no reason to feel that you're not a true "Gardnerian" or "Alexandrian."

Sure, you're a solitary practitioner rather than a coven member, but why should that matter?

Avoiding the Endless "Label" Debates

Actually, to be frank, there are plenty of "orthodox" coven members who will tell you that it does matter, but they're speaking from their own perspective.

Many coveners still believe that it takes an initiated witch to make another witch, at least in their particular tradition. Yet solitary practitioners following these traditions will usually undertake a self-initiation, which they often describe as one of the most sacred and special experiences in their lifetime.

The fact is, no one has the authority to decree that one person is a Wiccan—Gardnerian or otherwise—and another is not.

It's true that self-initiation is seen as a sort of minimum requirement that one would want to have completed before calling oneself a Wiccan—just as you most likely wouldn't call yourself a Catholic unless you'd been converted and baptized into the faith.

Nonetheless, there's no one handing out "Wiccan certificates" to make your solitary practice official.

Covens can deny you initiation into their group, and it's their right to do so. But if you're choosing the solitary path, then you probably wouldn't have wanted to join them anyhow. (And even if the choice is only based on a lack of covens in your area, you might consider the possibility that you're actually meant for the solitary path.)

In the grand scheme of things, when it comes to "covens versus solitaries" or any other perceived point of debate among the huge diversity of Wiccans out there, mutual respect remains the ideal.

Don't get embroiled in arguments on the Internet (or in person) if you don't want to get bogged down in negative energy. No matter what path you choose in the Wiccan world, you know who you are, and no one else can tell you differently unless you let them.

MOVING FORWARD

Now that we've covered the differences between the coven life and the solitary path, and the benefits of each, it's time to take a look at some of the traditions you might choose from as you continue your explorations.

In the next sections, we'll briefly review some of the major traditions under the Wiccan umbrella. As always, pay attention to the signals your sixth sense sends to you as you read—it may be that a specific tradition jumps out at you right away, asking you to explore it further.

If this doesn't happen, no worries! It's still useful to have some background knowledge of available options as you seek your path.

SECTION TWO

WICCAN TRADITIONS

THE MOST POPULAR WICCAN TRADITIONS

You may already know that the term "Wicca" was never used by Gerald Gardner himself. Gardner referred to himself and his Bricket Wood coven members as "the Wica," but had no name beyond "witchcraft" in reference to their activities. "Wicca" didn't actually become a widely-recognized term until several years later.

Furthermore, Gardner never used the term "Gardnerian"—this was actually coined by another witch, Robert Cochrane, who ran in some of the same circles as Gardner back in the mid-20th century. Cochrane practiced his own form of the Craft and used "Gardnerian" as a way of distinguishing his own work from Gardner's.

This is all to say that what we think of as established terminology can have almost accidental origins. It's also a glimpse into how traditions are often born—by the splitting off of one or more practitioners from an established tradition into a new way of doing things.

Even within established traditions, such as Gardnerianism, there can be different branches practicing in slightly different ways, and as discussed above, every coven will have its own unique approach to the work. But there are still pretty clear boundaries between one tradition of Wicca and another.

Below, we'll take a look at three major limbs of the "tree" of Wicca—the Gardnerian, Alexandrian, and Dianic traditions—as these are the three you're most likely to encounter at the beginning of your exploration of this diverse religion.

THE GARDNERIAN TRADITION

Obviously, the Gardnerian Tradition is the oldest form of what we now call Wicca, having been developed in the 1950s, though some might argue that it originated with the witches Gerald Gardner trained under prior to creating his first magic compendium (High Magic's Aid) and creating the Bricket Wood Coven.

Gardner certainly attributed much of what he taught in his coven to a handful of witches belonging to what was called the New Forest Coven in the UK, but this isn't widely documented so it's hard to assert with confidence.

We do know that Gardner drew some of his information and inspiration from Aleister Crowley's works and the teachings of the Hermetic Order of the Golden Dawn, so there is consensus that the Gardnerian Tradition follows something older than the 20th century, in a combined form newly presented by Gardner.

Gardnerian Wiccans traditionally work in covens of 13 members, although this number can vary depending on the circumstances of the group. It's an initiatory tradition, meaning that one can only be initiated through another Gardnerian witch, so that every "true" Gardnerian can trace his or her lineage back to Gardner's original coven.

Gardner was an enthusiastic practitioner of nudism, which is where this element of the tradition came from, and the more orthodox Gardnerian covens today still practice ritual nudity.

The coven is led by a High Priestess, with a High Priest as "second in command," and this gender polarity is particularly important, as it reflects the mythical story of the sabbats, with the God being the deity who dies and is reborn year after year, while the Goddess is eternally alive.

The Gardnerian deities are the Horned God and the Mother Goddess, and they have specific names that are supposed to be kept secret from non-initiates. There is a great deal of emphasis on using the original Book of Shadows that Gardner created for rituals and magic, which is also supposed to be kept secret, although it has been published in a few different forms over the decades. Gardnerian rituals are highly elaborate in comparison to rituals in other traditions, and traditionally involved ritual sex, although this may or may not happen in present-day covens.

The three degrees of initiation discussed above in the coven section originated here, though they are probably borrowed from the traditions of older secret societies like the Freemasons and The Golden Dawn. Gardnerian covens are among the most secretive, making this tradition, at least in coven form, difficult to navigate for newcomers and curious outsiders.

THE ALEXANDRIAN TRADITION

Founded during the 1960s as an addendum to Gardnerian Wicca, the Alexandrian Tradition differs slightly from the original tradition in some interesting ways.

It was created by Alex Sanders and his wife Maxine, who were members of the Gardnerian Tradition and initiated into one of its covens in the early 60s.

The tradition was named "Alexandrian" by a friend and fellow witch, Stewart Farrar, in part because of Sanders' first name, but also in veneration of the Library of Alexandria. Constructed in the 3rd Century in

Alexandria, Egypt, it was one of the first libraries in the world and housed a wealth of occult knowledge.

The Alexandrian Tradition is extensively covered in books by Stewart and Janet Farrar, authors and Wiccan practitioners who were both initiated into the main coven of the tradition by Maxine Sanders herself back in the 70s.

Alexandrian Wicca is similar to Gardnerian Wicca in many ways.

The High Priestess is the head of the coven, and there is a belief in the Goddess as well as a God. They also observe the three degrees of membership in a coven, although it differs slightly.

In terms of the worship of deities, however, there's an interesting twist: the Alexandrian Tradition follows the tale of the Holly King and his counterpart, the Oak King. Like the Gardnerian version, this tale is an ever-revolving wheel that coincides with the wheel of the year and explains the nature of each Wiccan sabbat perfectly:

The Oak King is born and conquers the dying Holly King. The Oak King then meets up with the maiden aspect of the Goddess in the early part of the year. They marry, and then the Goddess is impregnated. The Oak King comes to the height of his power during the Midsummer celebration, and the Goddess is ready to come into her mother form. As the Oak King's power begins to wane, we see the birth of the Holly King, who eventually slays the Oak King as the Goddess comes into her crone aspect during Midwinter.

Other differences between Gardnerian Wicca and Alexandrian Wicca include the choice to practice in clothing or ritual wear, and the presence of ceremonial magic and Hermeticism.

The tradition isn't necessarily quite as secretive or dogmatic. While there is some emphasis on the need to "follow the book" and its main teachings, there is a greater emphasis on growth and living out your own path, allowing for many changes and adjustments as practitioners see fit.

THE DIANIC TRADITION

Dianic Wicca takes a rather big departure from the older Wiccan traditions, and may be the first to come out of the United States rather than the UK.

The original and most well-known form of the tradition was founded in the 1970s by a woman named Zsuzsanna Budapest.

This is an all-female tradition, with a cosmology that focuses solely on the supremacy of the Goddess. As such, those who learn and study Dianic Wicca will mostly be monotheistic in a matriarchal system. There is an emphasis in this tradition on being politically and socially aware of the oppression and injustices faced by women.

This tradition typically does not have a hierarchical structure and is much freer in terms of spiritual growth and movement within the coven.

As in other traditions, Dianic Wiccans will meet on esbats, sabbats, and other significant times such as when a member or someone in the community is in need, but the work within these circles is very fluid and follows a woman-based approach in all things. There is a great deal of focus on emotional support here, and it isn't uncommon to find that women have entered Dianic covens or circles in order to heal themselves from some trauma or personal issue surrounding their femininity.

Another form of Wicca sharing the name "Dianic" was later started by Morgan McFarland and her husband, Mark Roberts, and this tradition does admit men, as do other traditions inspired by the original Dianic Wicca. However, those initiated through Budapest remain female-only.

A word of caution about the Dianic Traditions is that some practitioners will condone malevolent magic against those who harm women or cause them injustice through hexes, curses, and bindings. This is not a majority, however—most modern-day Dianic Wiccans will follow The Rede and Threefold Law.

OTHER TRADITIONS WITHIN THE WICCAN WORLD

The Gardnerian, Alexandrian, and Dianic Traditions may be the most widely practiced established traditions today, but there are many others, all with varying degrees of similarity to the older traditions.

One quite prominent tradition is Seax-Wica, a direct descendant of Gardnerian Wicca with an arguably more "American" feel, whose founder is often credited with bringing Wicca to the United States.

In more recent decades, several "cultural" forms have emerged that draw exclusively from a specific pantheon, rather than borrowing a Goddess from one pantheon and a God from another, which is fairly common in covens following the older traditions.

These "ethnic" traditions aim to translate the more "standard" Wiccan beliefs and practices into more culturally relevant forms in various ways.

We'll introduce two of these below, along with a final NeoPagan tradition that can be found across several forms of Wicca, and so deserves a mention here.

This is by no means an exhaustive list of Wiccan traditions, of course, but a brief overview of some of the more common forms that have taken root since the latter part of the twentieth century.

SEAX-WICA

Seax-Wica was also founded in the U.S. in the 1970s, by a British-born witch named Raymond Buckland.

Buckland had been a High Priest in the Gardnerian Tradition—the first in the U.S.—and started the first Gardnerian coven after moving to New York in the early 1960s.

After a decade of leading his Long Island Coven, however, he was growing more and more disenchanted with the way the hierarchical structure of Gardnerianism created politics and ego-battles in American initiates. He founded Seax-Wica as a way of continuing what was useful about Gardnerianism but in a fashion that was more suited to the culture of his new home.

Seax-Wica is inspired by Anglo-Saxon witchcraft as it was practiced in Anglo-Saxon England between the 5th and 11th centuries.

Its main deities are Woden and Freya, who represent the God and Goddess as found in the original Gardnerian Tradition. All the sabbats and esbats are celebrated. There is an emphasis on studying herbal lore and several forms of divination, including the Tarot and the Runes.

There are many differences between Seax-Wica and the more orthodox forms of Wicca.

For starters, there is no oath of secrecy, so it's not such a challenge to find out what goes on in covens, how they approach their rituals, etc. In fact, Buckland wrote a book, originally called The Tree and now republished as Buckland's Book of Saxon Witchcraft that serves as a guide to the tradition for any who would like to explore it. (It should be noted that this particular book assumes the reader already has a working knowledge of Wicca. If you don't, then be sure to check out Buckland's The Complete Book of Witchcraft to help you fill in the gaps.)

Furthermore, rituals and sabbat celebrations can be open, if the coven so chooses.

There is no Book of Shadows in this tradition, and adding new material to rituals, magic, etc. is welcomed if practitioners see fit.

There are no degrees of advancement as there are in other traditions, and coven leaders are democratically elected, serving a term of one lunar year (13 full moons). There is also no emphasis on lineage—in other words, being initiated by another Seax-Wica witch is not necessary. Self-dedication is recognized as a perfectly acceptable entry point to this form of the Craft.

NORSE WICCA

Just as Seax-Wica takes its inspiration from Anglo-Saxon pagan practices, Norse Wicca is infused with the beliefs, practices, and deities of the ancient Norse traditions of Scandinavia.

There is even a potential for some overlap between these two forms, since the pre-Christian Anglo-Saxon culture shares Germanic roots with the Norse culture of Scandinavia, and many similarities have been between the religions of the two areas—though it should be noted that more is known about the old Norse religion than about its Anglo-Saxon counterpart. And although Christianity did its best to eradicate these traditions, just as it did throughout pagan Europe, remnants of this rich culture are still with us today, in the form of Easter eggs, Christmas trees, and even five of our seven days of the week, named for Norse deities.

Unlike Seax-Wica, Norse Wicca is not an "official" tradition with a single founder, but rather an emerging trend among Wiccans who wish to work with a specific pantheon of deities and may draw inspiration from the ancient Norse sagas such as the Eddas and the Grimnismal. It's also common to adopt Germanic and Norse versions of sabbats, such as celebrating the Horse Fest at the Autumnal Equinox (often known as Mabon in traditional Wicca).

Working with runes is one element that many Norse Wiccans have in common with those in the Seax tradition. Runes originated in this culture as far back as 150 AD, and are thought to have served as both letters of an alphabet and magical talismans. Divination with runes is common among many NeoPagan paths, including other forms of Wicca.

One chief difference between what we might call "standard" or traditional Wicca and the Norse-influenced form is the potential for a richer and more nuanced sense of the afterlife. Indeed, the Norse religious belief system has a dense complexity that can make Wicca's beliefs and tenets seem rather two-dimensional in comparison. However, many followers of Norse Wicca adopt a syncretic approach, weaving the elements of the Norse system that resonate with them into their personal practice. Norse Wiccans tend to be solitary practitioners, with known covens being rather few and far between.

Norse Wicca should not be confused with Pagan reconstructionist religions such as Asatru or Odinism, whose followers aim to practice Norse religion as it truly existed in pre-Christian times. These reconstructionists, or "recons" for short, work only from verifiable historical sources, and actively distinguish their practice from that of Wiccans.

CELTIC WICCA/DRUIDIC WICCA

Also based in the belief system of an ancient world, Celtic Wicca and Druidic Wicca are technically two different traditions, though many Wiccans incorporate elements of both in their practice.

The Druids were the priestly class of Celtic society, serving as healers, poets, and philosophers, who practiced divination and magic as part of their role. Therefore, they were part of the fabric of Celtic life, and separating them out in order to practice strictly "Celtic Wicca" is definitely missing an important part of the picture.

Celtic Wiccans obviously work with deities of the Celtic pantheon—whether Irish, Welsh, Cornish, or even Gaulish (like the Germanic cultures, the Celts occupied a wide territory), and use Celtic names for sabbats, such as Lughnassa instead of Lammas.

The Ogham—a Celtic runic system—may be used in magical symbolism and divination, and some practitioners adopt the Celtic classification of elements rather than the standard Wiccan system.

Celtic covens may or may not involve a hierarchy or degrees of advancement—it depends on how much of Gardnerian or Alexandrian Traditions they wish to incorporate into their syncretic form of the Craft.

As for Druidic Wiccans, there is generally a focus on viewing all of nature as inherently divine, and all things as connected.

There is more of a metaphysical and shamanistic bent than what is found in more traditional Wicca. Animals are important to this belief system, particularly the stag, the salmon, the raven, the boar, and several others indigenous to ancient Ireland.

An emphasis on herbal magic and sacred stones is also often part of this tradition.

Again, hierarchy may or may not be present in Druidic covens, but there is a greater likelihood of a more egalitarian structure than that found in more traditional Wicca.

Almost nothing is known about the specific magical and/or religious activities of the Druids, since they deliberately kept their knowledge in an oral tradition, so much of what is practiced today is inspired from Celtic mythology and the roles Druids play in these stories.

Most of what we know from written sources comes from a Christianized lens through monks recording the lore in medieval Ireland, and a solid amount from Celtic

Wales has also survived, so Celtic and Druidic Wicca tend to have distinctly Irish and Welsh influences.

There are counterparts to the Norse Asatru and Odinism groups in this part of the world in the form of modern day "NeoDruids," as well as Celtic Reconstructionists. Both groups also distinguish themselves from Wicca, which is, of course, a religion of entirely modern origin, as opposed to a pre-Christian way of life being "reconstructed" in contemporary times.

FAERY WICCA

Faery Wicca is more of an umbrella term than a tradition in its own right. It refers to an element of the belief systems of several different paths within the Craft, which is the incorporation of fairy folklore and the active alignment with spirit entities called faeries (also spelled "fairies"). These beings can take a multitude of forms depending on the traditions they come from, but are often depicted as resembling humans.

Although faeries are most often associated with Celtic culture, they are not limited to this realm—belief in spirits that we would translate as "faeries" exists in ancient and contemporary cultures all over the globe.

In the English-speaking Faery traditions, they tend to be collectively referred to as "the fey." These earth-spirits are often associated with forests and hilly landscapes, and retain a surprisingly active presence in local folklore in rural Ireland and Scotland.

Wiccans who practice a Faery faith may call on these beings during spellwork, but there is a range of opinion on what kinds of magical aims faeries can be counted on to assist with.

Their personalities are generally not considered to be necessarily friendly toward humans (indeed, Peter Pan's Tinkerbell is pretty much an exception to the rule), although this can depend on circumstances, including whether or not the practitioner has offered or said something to get the fairies "on their side."

For example, it is believed that you can plant a garden or leave out items that will attract certain sprites into your yard or home. Because of the emphasis on working with spirits, Faerie Wicca is considered to be among the more shamanic practices on the Wiccan spectrum. Those who work this type of magic often work with oils, herbs, flowers, and other tools directly sourced from nature.

Faery Wicca is not the same as the Feri Tradition of witchcraft, which is a non-Wiccan form of the Craft developed in the mid-20th century in the United States by Victor and Cora Anderson. In fact, their tradition was initially called the Faery Tradition, but they changed the spelling to "Feri" in order to avoid being confused with the ever-growing number of Wiccan and other NeoPagan groups using the word "Faery" (or "Fairy") to identify themselves.

SECTION THREE
ECLECTIC WICCA

INTRODUCTION TO ECLECTIC WICCA

As you can see, there is quite a variety of potential paths for Wiccans to follow, whether they are solitary practitioners or initiates in a coven.

Ever since the days of Gardner and his first initiated witches, followers of the Craft have been innovating and adapting their practices to better suit their circumstances, their areas of interest, and their inner spiritual compasses, effectively creating new multiple traditions with each generation of Wiccans. And now that the phenomenon of solitary practice has become such a mainstay, it's become very common for individual Wiccans to create their own unique practices out of a sort of "patchwork" of many traditions, while also adding elements of their own invention.

Indeed, you could almost call "Eclecticism" its own "tradition" within Wicca, except that the only thing eclectic practices truly have in common with each other is that they're different from every other practice. In other words, the only tradition of eclecticism is independent thought and a willingness to be a spiritual pioneer, forging one's own path to a unique Wiccan practice.

The degree to which eclectic Wiccans "invent" their form of the religion (and not all Wiccans in this category would even necessarily agree with the term "religion") depends on the individual. Some might create highly unique ritual structures completely from their own inspiration and imagination, while others might simply blend Gardnerian and Dianic approaches, with little to no original material added in.

So you can see why it's essentially impossible to provide any specific information about the practice of eclecticism.

ECLECTIC SOLITARY PRACTICE

It's fair to say that the vast majority of eclectic Wiccans are solitary practitioners.

As discussed earlier, when you're practicing solo, you have the ultimate say in which direction, or directions, you'd like to explore along your spiritual path. While many solitaries do, in fact, choose to follow one specific tradition, it's probably the case by now that a majority of solitaries are eclectic in their practice.

One possible reason for this ever-rising trend is the wonderful diversity of perspectives offered in print and online sources about Wicca.

Solitary readers with no local Wiccan community to participate in are left with no other choice but to read, and (ideally) read widely, and in doing so, will find differing, and even conflicting, ideas about Wiccan philosophy, beliefs, and elements of ritual practice.

After some amount of initial exploration in this way, a solitary aspiring Wiccan will likely either feel drawn to a particular tradition and therefore keep pursuing sources that are part of that tradition, or feel somewhat uncertain about how to proceed. Those who feel uncertain will continue to read widely, and more likely than not, will cobble their own "traditions" together for themselves, with the help of the sources they resonate best with.

Another potential motivator for pursuing an eclectic path is the deity aspect of Wicca.

It can be a real stretch for those new to the faith, and particularly for those who were raised in one of the monotheistic religions (particularly Christianity) to suddenly be able to believe in a pagan deity from Greece or Egypt or Ireland who has, up until this point in their lives, been only a mythical character in stories, or else entirely unheard of.

Eclectic Wiccans can take a more gradual, individualized approach to the issue of deity. Perhaps the more generalized Goddess and God are easier for some to wrap their minds around. Or, perhaps there are one or two specific deities that make particular spiritual sense for a would-be traditionalist, but that aren't recognized by any traditions.

It's often said that relationships with deities must be cultivated over time—that you can't just automatically start believing in Isis just because your High Priestess insists that Isis exists. In eclectic practice, there's more room for forging one's own sense of what it means to worship a deity, and to come up with one's own language for describing it.

Of course, with eclectic solitary practice comes the challenge of essentially having to be your own teacher. You can read all you like—and you should—but at the end of the day, there's no one to guide you to your next step, because you're truly forging your own path.

Thankfully, we now have the possibility of virtual community via the Internet, and there's no shortage of people blogging, commenting, and otherwise chatting away about all things Wiccan, so you don't have to be completely solo if you don't want to be.

But if you're not following a specific tradition, then you have many, many more decisions to make on your own, and for some people, this gets overwhelming.

The best thing to do, if you're just starting out and you're unsure, is to read as much as you can, paying attention to what resonates with you as you do so, and let your heart lead you to the next step along the path.

ECLECTIC COVENS

It may almost seem like an oxymoron, but eclectic covens do exist.

After all, not all Wiccans who wish to be eclectic in their practice also wish to be solitary. An eclectic coven can be a wonderful place to find like-minded, independent spiritual companions with enough in common to make a well-functioning, diverse religious community.

The degree of uniqueness in any given eclectic coven will depend on why and how the coven was formed. For example, groups falling in this category may form because they believe in a blended cosmology—specific deities from a number of different pantheons—that don't fit neatly with any existing tradition. Beyond the deities of choice, the practice of such a coven may very closely emulate one of the more established traditions, but the more orthodox followers of that tradition will view the coven following a blended cosmology as "eclectic."

Other covens will deviate further from an existing tradition by merging it more extensively with another tradition.

While every single detail of the practice may belong to one of the established traditions, the fact that they are mixed together makes the coven "eclectic" rather than traditional.

Interestingly, this is often how new traditions get started. For instance, both Algard and Georgian Wicca are blends of the Alexandrian and Gardnerian Traditions with other elements mixed in, and each now has several covens practicing under their names.

Sometimes the move into eclecticism is gradual, rather than decisively chosen. For example, over time, some covens gradually adapt their practice to the extent that they're really no longer adhering to the basic tenets of the tradition they started out under.

An example of this would be if a coven was originally following the Dianic Tradition but decided to allow men access to the coven, and/or elected to worship a God in addition to a Goddess. The tradition cannot be called Dianic anymore—in the original sense—because the veneration of the Goddess has been sublimated and men are allowed to access the faith. (As noted above, there are now covens who identify as Dianic but don't emphasize the feminine, but for the purpose of this example, we're talking about the original Dianic Tradition.)

Finally, there are some covens that are deliberately and wildly eclectic from the very start, encouraging a diversity of practices among their members, provided that all involved will hold a few basic tenets in common.

These basic tenets are usually about ethics—tolerance for other paths, harm to none, etc. Within these groups, subgroups may form that have enough in common to move off on their own and solidify their own new traditions. Again, this is in keeping with the overall nature of Wicca over time—constant adaptation, evolution, and growth.

ECLECTIC CIRCLES

As mentioned earlier in this guide, Wiccan circles tend to be eclectic by design.

The great thing about this is that solitaries wishing to join a circle can be followers of a tradition or eclectic, and it doesn't matter either way.

In fact, some circles function as study groups who will take turns exploring different traditions, offering opportunities to build an eclectic practice for those interested in doing so.

If you're leaning toward eclecticism as opposed to following a specific tradition, and looking to commune and practice with others at least some of the time, then a circle is likely to be the most practical option for you.

MAKING PEACE WITH TRADITION

The term "eclectic" has essentially come out of the need to recognize, within the Wiccan community, that there are those who are going to stick to tradition and those who are not.

As mentioned above, there are plenty of Gardnerian and Alexandrian initiates (as well as those initiated in Seax Wicca, Dianic Wicca, etc.) who do not believe that a Wiccan can be self-initiated or be a solely solitary practitioner. Their traditions are sacred to them and while they don't necessarily begrudge other people following their own paths, they do mind it when said people call their path "Wicca."

One term sometimes used to describe those who don't follow coven-centered Gardnerian or Alexandrian Wicca is "NeoWiccan."

This is somewhat similar to the use of "NeoPagan" to distinguish those who currently follow Pagan practices today from those who worshipped "pagan" deities in the first centuries of the rise of Christianity. The Pagan practices of today may be based on and inspired by what we know of earlier times, but they are definitely not the same.

In this sense, "NeoWiccan" is a fair analogy, since eclectics and solitaries are not, in fact, practicing what

Gardner and Alex Sanders practiced with their covens. The main difference is that "original" paganism happened literally centuries ago, and original Wicca has been around for far less than a century.

Furthermore, as has been stated several times already in this guide, Wicca has always been a dynamic, ever-changing religion since the beginning—both Gardner and Sanders continually revised their covens' Books of Shadows, adapting their practices as they went along.

So, while "NeoWiccan" makes sense to some—and some practitioners are happy to adopt the label for themselves—the more commonly used term is "eclectic," as it speaks to the nature of the people who pursue this type of path.

FOLLOW YOUR HEART

Again, the great thing about Wicca is that no one can tell you that you must join a coven, that you must practice alone, or that you must (or must not) follow a specific tradition. You get to decide for yourself.

However, you should definitely give yourself plenty of time to make this choice, and you should always remain open to the possibility that your decision could change over time.

Becoming an eclectic Wiccan, with all the freedom that "eclectic" implies, can sound like an enticing prospect, and it can be a very rewarding path for some. But it is only with serious soul-searching and study that you will find your true path of practice, so don't rule out the other traditions and modes of worship simply because being an eclectic witch sounds like a walk in the park.

If anything, it can be more difficult, because of the above-mentioned lack of comprehensive guidance and training from other Wiccans. But for those who truly feel called to eclecticism, many people describe it as a very liberating, personal path of spirituality that is no less sacred than following a single tradition.

SECTION FOUR
FINDING YOUR PATH

THE NEXT STEPS

The scope of Wiccan practice is quite impressive when we look at all the various ways in which it is followed. But given all the choices, it might actually be more difficult these days for interested beginners to find their way forward.

The first thing to remember is that it will probably take a while before you find your comfort zone within the Craft.

The tradition within Wicca of studying for a year and a day before being eligible for initiation into a coven speaks to the depth of the learning process. (In fact, plenty of covens will tell you that you're not necessarily ready to make that leap after only a year and a day.)

So take your time. And in the meantime, here are some suggestions for how you might take your next steps.

READ, READ, AND READ SOME MORE

Research is the best thing you can do in order to gain an informed sense of the Craft and where your path into it might be found.

You're already well on your way there if you're reading this book, and this is just the tip of the iceberg when it comes to print and online resources.

Look into the things that you do not understand. Pursue further anything that really catches your interest. When you come across something that doesn't give you a good feeling—a belief, a practice, a particular author's take on things—take note of it, and see if you can sort out why it doesn't resonate with you. Understanding what you don't want helps you clarify what it is you're truly looking for.

You should be prepared to read several books, and blogs, if you're so inclined, on the topic of Wicca in your early days, and you should also resolve to never stop learning about it.

STUDY THE TRADITIONS

One of the easiest ways to figure out which type of practice is best suited to you is through studying the main Wiccan traditions. Again, it can be a challenge to find specific, detailed information about rites and rituals, etc., due to the traditions many orthodox covens have about keeping their knowledge secret.

If approaching a traditional coven isn't possible or just isn't your cup of tea, look up the traditions online, read books about them, and notice how you feel about each of them when you learn what they are about and how they operate. (You might start at the very beginning with Gardner's work, High Magic's Aid.)

If you find that they are unappealing to you in some way, discard the notion of joining that specific tradition or worshiping that specific pantheon.

Again, the point of it all is having an informed opinion, and that's gained through researching Wicca and its different paths.

FINDING THE RIGHT CIRCLE OR COVEN

Finding the circles and covens that operate in your area can be pretty close to impossible if you have no clue where to look.

While covens not looking for new members are unlikely to advertise their existence, some circles and Pagan groups use local media to announce meetings, ritual gatherings, etc. There are also online communities, forums, blogs, etc. that feature lists of covens and circles.

If you do find a directory of covens online, it will likely show what tradition the coven practices and how to contact a member or the High Priestess if they're looking for new members.

RESOURCES FOR SOLITARY WITCHES

Solitary practitioners who are new to the craft and do not have the guidance of other witches in their daily lives have to work a bit harder to find information.

In the Internet age, however, this is much less of a problem.

There are now countless resources out there for solo witches seeking guidance with spell-casting, rituals, and any other aspect of the faith. And, perhaps best of all, books can be ordered and delivered to those who don't have the luck to live in a community where such books might be sold.

Online Articles, Blogs, Videos, etc.

The Internet has indeed made it possible for the Wiccan community to be literally global.

There is probably no aspect of any tradition that hasn't been discussed online, and the diversity of voices from all over the world on any number of topics is truly astonishing.

There are some great blogs out there, and online videos can be wonderful resources for those who want to get closer to hands-on experience with ritual, etc. It's amazing what a good session with a search engine can do.

Of course, there's also a bunch of nonsense out there (this is the Internet we're talking about here, after all). There are writers with varying degrees of knowledge about their subject, and plagiarism runs rampant across many, many websites.

For example, one page on Wikipedia may be incredibly thorough, fact-checked, and well-written, while another on a related topic might be full of factual errors, or even completely made-up.

However, it's also fair to say that what constitutes "nonsense" to some will be perfectly legitimate and correct to others, and reading various sides of debates about traditionalism, etc. can be very insightful. But be a discerning reader, and evaluate your sources wisely.

If you're looking for a good starting point, I have just released my own website at **wiccaliving.com**. I also strongly recommend the excellent Celtic Connection resource, found at **Wicca.com**.

Online Forums and Message Boards

Online message boards, forums, and chat rooms can be a wonderful place to network with other Wiccans both in covens and outside of them. (And yes, there are even online covens!)

As mentioned above, these are excellent places to find out about covens and circles in your area and places near your location where there are meet-ups, but they also have great tips for ordering from online stores selling magical items and ritual tools, as well as general pleasant banter with like-minded folks.

Magazines and Newsletters

There have been magazines and newsletters on the Craft for decades and they're still, believe it or not, in existence.

Most are online now, offering websites with monthly or weekly updates and monthly newsletters via email, but print is not dead, so keep an eye out for the possibility of finding actual hard copies.

Books

Ah, good old-fashioned books.

Yes, books can still be the most comprehensive and focused resources for students of Wicca.

The best thing you can do to learn your Craft is amass a large collection of books on pantheons, traditions, spells, and magical correspondences.

One note to keep in mind here is that, like Internet sources, not all books are written by people with a solid education in the Craft. In the age of self-publishing, it's useful to check out whether a book has been published through a traditional publishing house, as those authors tend to be well-vetted and respected in the Wiccan community.

This doesn't mean that all self-published books are rubbish—some can be quite informative—but there is more of an issue of quality control.

CONCLUSION

By now, you should have a basic grasp of the myriad traditions and applications of Wiccan practice.

If you're interested in pursuing the Craft further, the next recommended step is—as you may have guessed—to keep reading!

Find as many resources as you can, both in print and online, and dive into what interests you. Remember that there is no certified "correct" path into Wicca. If you want to follow an established tradition, you will find resources to get you started. If you favor an eclectic practice, the possibilities are virtually endless.

If you're interested in socializing with other Wiccans, another possible next step is to investigate potential circles or covens in your area. If you find the right group of people, this can be a wonderful way to enter the Craft, and it will almost certainly accelerate your pace of learning.

Of course, if you have friends who have a budding interest in Wicca as well, you can always form a "beginner's" circle in which you can study and learn together. For that matter, you can start a circle of your own by posting an inquiry in a suitable local publication, or in an online forum.

As noted earlier, it is important to keep your wits about you when it comes to group worship activities with people you don't know well. This is particularly true for covens, but it's good advice for circles also.

Don't ever let any kind of social pressure cause you to stay in a situation you find uncomfortable, and don't hesitate to walk away from illegal or potentially harmful activities. Again, these instances are rare, but they are possible due to the powerful energy inherent in the Craft and its appeal to certain less-than-stable personalities.

Of course, it's not just the rare instance of dodgy ulterior motives on the part of some who purport to be Wiccans that you should be on the lookout for. Pay attention to how the group energy feels, socially, as well. If you don't see yourself getting along well with one or more members of the group, then it might be pretty hard to relax into the learning and growth that these organizations are supposed to be providing.

Granted, most people take some getting used to, so don't dismiss a potential opportunity based solely on first impressions (unless the impression is really strong). Give others a chance, remembering that all friendships take time, while also being sure to be true to yourself.

As I always repeat at the end of my books: With Wicca, there is no right or wrong. This is especially true when you have such a diverse set of paths before you, and no one path is "better" than another.

Indeed, the most important thing that you can do when seeking your path to travel is to follow your intuition. If, as you learn about a specific tradition, its philosophies and tenets and feel that it resonates deep within your heart, you're home.

If, on the other hand, you notice any little red flags coming up for you, pay attention to them. Spirituality should feel good in your whole being. If ritual feels like a chore, or something feels "off" in any other way, you're not quite in the right place.

Finally, remember that finding your path is bound to take some time. Adopting any new religion requires plenty of study and consideration, so don't be concerned if it takes several months or longer for you to feel you've started to get your footing. And even should you decide to become an initiate, whether through coven or solitary practice, you should never stop seeking new knowledge.

I will leave you with that parting thought. It has been an absolute pleasure writing this book, and I hope you have enjoyed reading it. I wish you all the best on your journey, whichever route you take, and I hope that you find your practice rewarding.

Thank you one more time for reading.

Blessed Be.

SUGGESTIONS FOR FURTHER READING

As emphasized several times throughout this guide, those who want to become Wiccans need to be willing to study the Craft extensively. This study ideally goes on throughout your life as a Wiccan, but you will find that reading as much as you can at the beginning will help you get a solid grounding in the many traditions, beliefs, and practices of Wicca.

Below is a very brief list of recommended books that beginners will find accessible. Information about covens, solitary practice, and many of the Wiccan traditions covered in this guide can be found in one or more of these resources, along with many other topics. You can find these books online and in Wiccan, Pagan, or other "New Age" shops. Happy reading!

Scott Cunningham, *Wicca: A Guide for the Solitary Practitioner* (1989)

Raymond Buckland, *Buckland's Complete Book of Witchcraft* (1986)

Gary Cantrell, *Wiccan Beliefs & Practices: With Rituals for Solitaries & Covens* (2001)

Phyllis Currott, *Witch Crafting* (2001)

Gerald Garner, *Witchcraft Today* (1954, 2004)

DID YOU ENJOY *WICCA FINDING YOUR PATH*?

Again let me thank you for purchasing and reading my guide. There are a number of great books on the topic, so I really appreciate you choosing my guide.

If you enjoyed the book, I'd like to ask for a small favor in return. If possible, I'd love for you to take a couple of minutes to leave a review for this book on Amazon.

Your feedback will help me to make improvements to this guide, as well as writing books on other topics that might be of interest to you. Hopefully this will allow me to create even better guides in future!

OTHER BOOKS BY LISA CHAMBERLAIN

Wicca for Beginners: A Guide to Wiccan Beliefs, Rituals, Magic, and Witchcraft

Wicca Herbal Magic: A Beginner's Guide to Practicing Wiccan Herbal Magic, with Simple Herb Spells

Wicca Book of Spells: A Book of Shadows for Wiccans, Witches, and Other Practitioners of Magic

Wicca Book of Herbal Spells: A Book of Shadows for Wiccans, Witches, and Other Practitioners of Herbal Magic

Wicca Candle Magic: A Beginner's Guide to Practicing Wiccan Candle Magic, with Simple Candle Spells

Wicca Crystal Magic: A Beginner's Guide to Practicing Wiccan Crystal Magic, with Simple Crystal Spells

Wicca Moon Magic: A Wiccan's Guide and Grimoire for Working Magic with Lunar Energies

Wicca Essential Oils Magic: A Beginner's Guide to Working with Magical Oils, with Simple Recipes and Spells

Wicca Elemental Magic: A Guide to the Elements, Witchcraft, and Magical Spells

Tarot for Beginners: A Guide to Psychic Tarot Reading, Real Tarot Card Meanings, and Simple Tarot Spreads

Wicca Magical Deities: A Guide to the Wiccan God and Goddess, and Choosing a Deity to Work Magic With

Wicca Wheel of the Year Magic: A Beginner's Guide to the Sabbats, with History, Symbolism, Celebration Ideas, and Dedicated Sabbat Spells

Wicca Living a Magical Life: A Guide to Initiation and Navigating Your Journey in the Craft

Magic and the Law of Attraction: A Witch's Guide to the Magic of Intention, Raising Your Frequency, and Building Your Reality

Wicca Altar and Tools: A Beginner's Guide to Wiccan Altars, Tools for Spellwork, and Casting the Circle

Wicca Finding Your Path: A Beginner's Guide to Wiccan Traditions, Solitary Practitioners, Eclectic Witches, Covens, and Circles

Wicca Book of Shadows: A Beginner's Guide to Keeping Your Own Book of Shadows and the History of Grimoires

Modern Witchcraft and Magic for Beginners: A Guide to Traditional and Contemporary Paths, with Magical Techniques for the Beginner Witch

FREE GIFT REMINDER

I'd hate for you to miss out, so here is one final reminder of the free, downloadable eBook that I'm giving away to my readers.

Wicca: Little Book of Wiccan Spells is ideal for any Wiccans who want to start practicing magic. It contains a collection of ten spells that I have deemed suitable for beginners.

You can download it by visiting:

www.wiccaliving.com/bonus

I hope you enjoy it.

Made in the USA
Middletown, DE
16 January 2018